12

8795

D1784899

# INTRODUCTION

It has recently been estimated that there are at least two million adult illiterates in this country. Some think that there are probably more at various stages of reading development. Some will be completely illiterate but many more will be not quite 'functionally literate'. This means to have the ability to develop reading skills and vocabulary for oneself, using books such as dictionaries, without outside help.

The students who are striving to reach the level of functional literacy will come from all age groups, all social backgrounds, and will have many and varied interests. It is therefore not appropriate to provide a comprehensive scheme for these people as their needs and abilities vary so much. The strength of the tutorial system is that individual attention is possible for each student. This handbook aims to help the tutor to assess the nature of the student's problem, and to help in the planning of the programme for the student. It is most important that evaluation of progress is built into any programme of this sort, but this must not become onerous, or an end in itself. It is also important to avoid long reports but to consult frequently with your Organiser or Co-ordinator about difficulties in the reading situation and any problems which your student may have. If you are a teacher you will understand the importance of lesson preparation, and that for every hour of teaching one hour of preparation must be allowed.

Teaching adult non-readers can be demanding but rewarding work both for the tutor who has had no teacher training and also for the experienced teacher. This Handbook has been written with the needs of both types of tutor in mind. The four sections cover planning and preparatory work *before* meeting the student; activities and skills to prepare for the early stages of reading, and a form of the language experience method; the planning, teaching and evaluation of the phonic element; suggestions for interest material and bibliographies for both student's and tutor's use.

Throughout, checklists help the tutor to assess the student's progress. If he is ready to move on to the next stage the 'guidelines' can be used to plan that part of the programme. Cross references relate to subjects covered in other parts of the book. The Handbook is therefore a practical aid. It is intended to help the tutor assess the student's needs, evaluate his progress, and plan a programme which will help him to reach the level of functional literacy.

# 1

## PROGRAMMING

### The First Session

Perhaps one of the most crucial stages in the development of the adult 'new reader' is the placing with the tutor who is to work with him or her over the coming months. As a tutor you may feel nervous and inadequate, or super confident, but always remember that your student is much more worried about the meeting than you are. I have even had a student who ran away from this first meeting. It is therefore important to plan this session as carefully and with as much detail as possible. Tutors who have been away from study for some time comment on the problems of coping with basic training courses. How much more difficult it must be for the non-reader, who has perhaps learned skills by imitation over a number of years, to concentrate for any length of time! Be prepared to work up gradually to the full session.

The adult memory of *school* and therefore *learning* will probably be of sitting and being told pearls of wisdom by *teacher*. He will therefore *expect* that you will *teach* him something during his first session. It is essential that this expectation is satisfied, and that something, however small, is actually taught.

### Early Information

If you are to be in a position to start teaching during your first session careful preparation with your organiser is essential. If your student has been interviewed you can expect your organiser to give you his details in a number of areas:

### CHECKLIST 1

*Personal Information*

1. Name, Address, Marital status, Age, etc.
2. General health and obvious physical and mental disabilities
3. History of reading experiences
4. Impressions of his family life
5. Social and emotional stability
6. Mental ability
7. History of learning disabilities

3

## Interest and Motivation

8. Apparent successes
9. Apparent failures
10. Place of work and position
11. Background and interests
12. Long and short term goals and objectives
13. Vocabulary

## Reading

14. What sort of material can he read?
15. Which words can he recognize?
16. Can he read aloud?
17. Does he understand what he has read?
18. Estimated reading level
19. Phonic check (if appropriate — see pp. 30-32)
20. Results of any Diagnostic Tests (if appropriate) see pp. 44

It is important to remember that this information will probably be impressions only. It will have been obtained in a short interview. Nevertheless it will be the basis of the early work which you will do with your student.

## Planning the Programme

It is inevitable that during his life your student will have been faced with one, or probably more, reading schemes. To face him at this stage with yet another scheme will do little for his battle to overcome feelings of frustration and failure. A more sound approach is to plan a programme which will incorporate elements of a number of schemes as and when appropriate to the student.

Any programme should include, at some time or other, the following elements:

1. The assessment of reading readiness (see checklists 3, 4 and 5) pp. 14-15)
2. The development of a basic sight vocabulary (see pp. 20-21)
3. The assessment of phonic readiness (see checklist 8 pp. 22-23)
4. Phonic work (see pp. 23 and 26-28)
5. Spelling (see pp. 32-35)
6. Comprehension skill development
7. Development of permanent reading habits

Numbers 6 and 7 in the above list must, like the development of handwriting, be practised from the earliest stages of the teaching of reading. Always ensure that the student understands what he has read. Help him to develop reading habits by planning with him the occasions when he will read between lessons, and keep a careful check that he is adhering to the plan.

During the early days you will be building *your* picture of the student. It is essential that you plan the initial programme, with your organiser, before tuition starts. This will be open to constant review, but you will know what you are aiming to do, and this will give both you and your student confidence.

## *Guidelines for planning your programme*

1. Start well *below* the actual reading level.
2. Develop self-confidence in your student by allowing him to experience many successes. Let him do things which he can do well.
3. Begin and end each lesson with activities which guarantee successful results.
4. Make your student aware that he *has* been successful.
5. Build on his interests and his desire to learn.
6. Keep variety in the programme so that interests and attention remain high.
7. Remember that one skill learnt is the basis of another skill.
8. Your programme must remain flexible.
9. Set objectives for individual lessons and for longer periods of time. Explain these objectives to your student.
10. Involve your student in the planning of the programme.
11. Too many new words cause confusion and prevent any of them being learned.
12. Build on *real* experiences that your student understands rather than abstract ones.
13. Write boldly and clearly, always using 'small' or lower-case letters during the early stages. Select printing in which the 'a' and 'g' are printed as they are usually written.
14. Give your student plenty of opportunity to develop his handwriting skills. In the early stages a large-face typewriter can be used — such as an Adler Gabrielle with a 6pt. Bulletin typeface.

## ASSESSMENT OF DIFFERENT TEACHING METHODS

Most methods for the teaching of reading can be placed into 3 groups: decoding, reading for meaning and multiple clue.

Examples of each group are:

*Decoding*

Alphabetic — the letter *names* are taught.

Phonic — the *sounds* of letters, and groups of letters, are taught (see pp. 22-32)

*Reading for meaning*

Look-and-say, or whole word — words are taught as a whole, often by flashing* the word on a card and saying the sound at the same time.

Whole sentence — complete sentences are taught, as in look-and-say, and by relating them directly to illustrations.

*Multiple Clue*

Linguistic — using the student's own phrases, words are taught in context, eliminating the possibilities until the word is found which fits the context (see language experiment method pp. 20-21)

In terms of teaching adults we can say that these methods, or versions of these methods, are the major ones in use. The i.t.a.* and 'words in colour' may be classified under Phonic approach. You may come across other methods, such as Montessori's, which will need to be evaluated in terms of being appropriate to your student. Reading schemes (e.g. Royal Road Readers — see p. 38) should be looked at, and the predominant method identified. This method should then be checked with the For and Against list, given below, to decide whether it is appropriate to your student's learning at the time.

## Teaching Reading Methods — For and Against

### *Alphabetic*

*For*

Letter recognition is developed as is left to right sequence. All the consonants, except h, q and w, contain their sound, or phoneme*, plus an extra vowel:— b-ee for b, s-ee for c, d-ee for d, g, p, t, v. eh-l for l, eh-m for m, n, f, s, x.

*Against*

The sequence of the alphabet may be confusing — e.g., b and d are near one another in placing, sound and shape.

*asterisked words and terms are included in the glossary at the end of the book.

6

There is a risk of loss of interest due to concentration on letter recognition.

The student may associate the letter with one specific sound. -t is like a hammer — this does not help when letters sound differently in words — e.g. pa<u>th</u>.

## *Phonic*

*For*

This method helps auditory perception, and visual-auditory discrimination (see pp. 11, 15)

It is a systematic method of learning letter sounds and develops an understanding of the ways in which sounds are blended to form words.

It helps independent, confident reading as a result of the ability to 'unlock' new words.

Words can be tried out to see if they 'fit'. The student does not need to wait to be told but can extend his vocabulary himself.

This method is therefore an economic way of teaching reading.

*Against*

Blending can be difficult if the student has auditory difficulties (see p. 11)

The irregularity of the English language leads to a very restricted vocabulary and an artificial style in structured reading material.

The ability to memorise a rule is *NOT* a measure of the ability to *use* it.

Most of the many rules have exceptions.

Drills can destroy interest.

## *Look-and-say, or whole word*

*For*

Meaningful words are used, often with a picture to provide a clue. If look-and-say is taught with pictorial clues, service words are taught separately — the, are, you, — as sight words*.

*Against*

Individual letters may be ignored, especially endings and middle vowels.

It can lead to guessing.

There is no way that a new word can be decyphered, the student becomes 'tutor-dependent'.

The student finds it difficult to differentiate between words of similar length and shape — e.g. bag, bog.

## Whole sentence

### For
Emphasis on sentence and phrase.
The sentence is meaningful; interests are important.
The importance of meaning and intonation when reading aloud is emphasized.

### Against
Individual words and letters may be left out.
Leads to random guessing without using clues.
Written language may be unfamiliar leading to dialect substitutions — 'we was' for 'we were'.
Letter/sound association is not developed.

## Linguistic

### For
Shows that written language can be the same as spoken language, by writing down and using what the student has said as reading material.
Encourages intelligent guessing within the context of a sentence which the student understands.
The student learns new words in context, not in isolation.
The letter combinations — e.g., -ough — become familiar in the written language.
Helps left to right direction.
Gives opportunities for language development with students who have 'poor language' difficulties (see p. 10).
Makes a story in his own language to which he can relate; not someone else's story.

### Against
Vocabulary may be uncontrolled.
Phonic skills may not be taught with continuity.
The student may not be given the opportunity to try to understand someone else's story.
Similar letter pattern forms can be confusing — e.g. same, cane, bane.
Differences in use of language may be under-rated.

It must be noted that these 'for' and 'against' lists are in relation to the adult new reader who is being taught by a tutor who may or may not be experienced in the teaching of reading. There is no doubt that millions of people have learned to read by the Alphabetic method, and that the Phonic method is scientifically sound and generally recognized if carefully and logically taught. Avoid discounting any reasonable method, and devise a programme which will build on and extend the strengths of your student, at particular times as he or she progresses. This programme must be flexible and will include elements of different methods at different times.

## ASSESSING READABILITY

If the student is being taught to read using unstructured material it is important that the level of difficulty of the material is assessed. This measure is frequently expressed in terms of Reading Age*. Many people now feel that it is inappropriate to refer to an adult in terms of 'being able to read as well as a child of seven'. His vocabulary may well involve the use of complex technical terms. It is perhaps more appropriate to discuss reading progress in terms of a more arbitrary scale. Readability can be assessed in many ways, but perhaps the one which is most appropriate to adults takes into account:

The average length of sentence

The percentage of difficult words.

The Fog Index[1] takes the above factors into account. The calculation is quite straightforward:

1. Mark a sample of 100 words from the middle of the book or passage.
2. Count the number of sentences.
3. Divide the number of words by the number of sentences to find the average number of words per sentence.
4. Count the number of 'hard words', i.e., words of three or more syllables.
5. Add (3) and (4) together and multiply by 0·4.

The Fog Index gives a scale from 1 to 23. Scale 6·8 roughly equates to Reading Age 6, and scale 10 to 11 is the level where functional literacy is achieved, equating roughly to Reading Age 9 to 10.

It is also important to take print size and format into account when assessing the suitability of material for your student.

[1] *The Technique of Reading* by R. Gunning, McGraw-Hill, 1952

# 2

## THE DIAGNOSIS OF READING FAILURE

The causes of reading problems are complex, and in any diagnosis it is important that we first understand the factors which are linked with reading disability.

## 1 Low Intelligence

People in the lower I.Q. ranges are not expected to acquire academic skills at the same rate as those of average ability. The same must also be true of reading. Just because one is *slow* to read does not mean that he is *unable* to read. Neither does *unable* to read mean that one is *stupid*. Allowances must always be made in the rate at which we expect our student to learn the skills related to reading.

## 2. Poor Language Development

The reasons for this factor may be listed in two groups: environmental problems and speech disabilities.

*Environmental problems.* Reading is interpreting language written down. Poor language development will lead to difficulties in reading. The most important time in a person's life, in terms of language development, is the pre-school period. If a child is not talked to, if books are not read to him, and the literate habit is not developed, this will affect him for much of his later life. I have also known the opposite situation to arise, where anxious parents attempted to instill the literate habit in a very young child by confronting him with many books and forcing him into a state of anxiety whenever books were shown to him. This young man was in his early twenties before he was able to conquer his literacy problems.

*Speech disabilities,* especially mouth and palate deformities, incomplete or ill-fitting teeth, cleft palate, etc. The tutor does not need to diagnose specific speech problems, but must be aware of the main areas of speech difficulty as these may have caused much embarrassment, emotional distress and withdrawal from reading activities in the past. These areas are:

- Those involving mispronunciation and lisping
- Difficulties in articulation
- Malformations, including incomplete or ill-fitting teeth.

In cases of severe difficulty a speech therapist must be consulted (see checklist 4 p. 15).

## 3. Physical Difficulties

Recurring illness may have led to long or frequent absences from school, and left the student unable to cope with the techniques of learning. Past failures may make him very tense in a learning situation. Inattention, rapid tiring, and a lack of ability to concentrate may be apparent.

Tutors are often surprised to learn of the importance of hearing in the teaching of reading but defective hearing can be a serious obstacle to learning to read. The auditory* abilities which are necessary are:

- Auditory perception — to be aware of different sounds.
- Auditory memory — to remember a sound which has been perceived.
- Auditory discrimination — to appreciate small similarities and differences between sounds.

It is possible to have adequate hearing but to have difficulty in differentiating between sounds. Some older students may have slight hearing losses (see checklist 3 nos. 5-7 p. 15).

The visual skills (see checklists 2, 3 (1-4) 5, pp. 14-15) which are necessary before reading can commence can be summarized as:

- To be aware of an image which has been drawn or written down.
- To be able to remember an image after it has been seen.
- To appreciate differences and similarities in shape and size and colour.
- To 'scan' or follow a line of print from left to right.

Problems which affect the ability to see properly fall into two areas: refractive and functional.

*Refractive problems,* such as long or short sight, astigmatism*, etc. Slight sight changes may occur in older students.

*Functional difficulties* affect the movement of the eye and depend on the muscles which control the eye. Reading consists of quick, short movements across the page, with frequent pauses, followed by a rapid sweep to the beginning of the next line. During these pauses the eye reacts to the images on the page. The frequency and duration of the pauses depend on the ability of the reader. This ability can never be taken for granted as students may reverse words or even omit lines at an early stage.

## 4 Left Handedness

This need not be a problem as many left-handed and adequate readers will testify. However, it may have led to untidy work as a result of the hand smudging and dirtying writing. As the work is written down it may be obscured by the hand passing over it, or the page being written on may be placed in front of the student instead of well to the left. These factors may produce 'poor visual feedback'. This means that the student has difficulty in recognizing, reading, and confirming in his mind what he has written. A further complication can be CROSS LATERALITY. Here a student who uses his left hand may 'line up' with his right eye. This is left hand/right eye dominant, or cross lateral. The student will place writing in front of his right eye instead of well to his left as indicated above. Neither factor is crucial in itself, but both can be important if other factors are involved.

## 5 Emotional and Personality Factors

These factors can be both *cause* and *effect* of reading difficulties. A child who suffers from emotional upsets as he grows up will face school and learning with anxiety. The result will be that he learns little; and frustration, discouragement and lack of interest lead directly to reading failure. It is important to remember that this could have been the case in your student's past. He may now regret past attitudes but you will still have to understand and help him to cope with the fears and anxieties with which he approaches learning in general, and reading in particular. You probably enjoy reading, and you must make sure that it is enjoyable for him too.

## 6 Home Background

Students who have had little or no experience with books during their early years may not see reading as important and therefore have little interest in acquiring its skills. It is only when some real need arises that true motivation* occurs. Lack of motivation may result from parental attitudes, and the habits of the child become the habits of the adult. It should be noted, however, that the vocabulary of many of our students is not limited, and is often
12

rich and colourful. It is *real* in every sense and we must take care *not to destroy* it. Our job as tutors is to extend the spoken language into one which is frequently written down and read. It is not our job to impose our own language, with all of its idiom and terminology, on our students. In the early days it may well be necessary to do a good deal of oral work in the form of talking with and reading to your student.

## 7 School Conditions

These are changing, and those which existed when many of our students were at school were very different from those which prevail today. Tutors may find it useful to visit local schools and observe the methods which are used to teach reading in their infant, primary and remedial departments.

## Summary

It is important to remember that reading failure is rarely the result of one single factor, but rather a combination of several. The basic assessment of the problem is a skilled job and will probably be undertaken by your organiser, co-ordinator or professional assessor. However, your work as a tutor will continually bring new factors to light, either confirming or altering the original diagnosis. Frequent consultation with your organiser is therefore essential if factors which are important are to be acted upon, and those factors which are not important ignored.

In the diagnosis of reading failure one must beware of the following dangers:

1. *Over generalizing* It is all too easy to apply a diagnostic test (see pp. 44-45) and to interpret the scores relying on the first symptom identified. All factors and results must be obtained and be seen as a 'picture' before making a definite final diagnosis.

2. *Non-recognition of professional boundaries* Whilst it is important that we are all aware of the factors which affect reading failure, we are not psychologists or doctors, least of all social workers. If we feel that our student has a specific problem in an area other than reading, we should seek the advice and opinion of our organiser or co-ordinator and discuss referral procedure. Of course we need to know, and be concerned about, social problems and home life, but our job is to *teach!* There is a counselling element to the work, but we are *not* guidance counsellors of any sort. The line is not an easy one to draw, but *beware over-involvement* as this leads to the student becoming too dependent on the

13

tutor for support in areas other than teaching.

*3 Bias* Care must be taken not to jump to conclusions, or to be drawn into collusion with your student against 'authority'. One student attempted to persuade me to help him to obtain some new shoes via his probation officer who was being unobliging! It would have been all too easy to have fallen into this trap.

## The assessment of specific reading problems

### CHECKLIST 2

*Visual problems which may be observed in a student with some small reading ability*
1.  Loses his place when reading
2.  Avoids close work
3.  Poor sitting position for reading and writing
4.  Holds reading material very close to his face
5.  Frequent blinking, frowning or scowling
6.  Many frequent head movements when reading
7.  Holds his body very rigidly when looking at distant objects
8.  Tends to rub his eyes
9.  Very tense when doing close work

If three or more of these signs are present consult your organiser with a view to obtaining the advice of an eye specialist.

### CHECKLIST 3

*Skills necessary before the student can begin to read*
1.  The ability to be aware of an image
● Daniels and Diack test of abstract figure (for Daniels and Diack see p. 45).
● Show black and white photographs and discuss.
2.  To be aware of differences and similarities in size shape and colour
● Test the use of words like: large – small, square – round, in relation to objects.
● Show a clear, boldly coloured picture. Does the student use words other than blue, red or green to describe the colours? Remember some students may be colour blind.
3.  The ability to recall an abstract image
● Show a picture and then cover it. Ask for a description and details.
4.  The ability to scan a line of print from left to right
● Use a maze similar to the one illustrated in *The Teaching of*

14

*Reading* by D. Moyle, pp. 137, 194.

5. The awareness of sounds
● Correct identification of recorded sounds such as a car, train, duck, aircraft, etc.
6. The appreciation of differences in sounds: questions such as:
● Which words sound the same at the end?

|      |       |      |     |
|------|-------|------|-----|
| cat  | dog   | bat  |     |
| bite | spoon | moon |     |
| gun  | fun   | fire | run |

● Which words sound the same at the beginning?

|       |       |      |      |
|-------|-------|------|------|
| bag   | ball  | lid  | bath |
| sheep | light | shoe | show |

7. The ability to remember a sound: ask the student to tell you some words beginning with b, f, d, etc.
8. An understanding of, and the ability to use, language
● Bring an object and talk about it.
● Tell a *short* story and ask your student to repeat it.
9. The ability to 'give attention' or concentrate during the lesson is important and can only be gauged from your own subjective impression of the student.

## CHECKLIST 4

*Assessment of speech disability*

1. Is there a lisp or stutter?
   Is s substituted by 1, th, sh?
2. Can the student make the following sounds? Failure to do so may indicate that he has articulation difficulties.

   ch, g, j, l, r, s, th(thick), th (thin), v, wh
3. Are the following substitutions made? If so, malformation of the mouth or ill-fitting teeth can be suspected, although regional variations must be taken into account.

| | | | |
|---|---|---|---|
| fing | — thing | date | — gate |
| vere | — there | bery | — very |
| tin | — thin | sink | — think |
| dat | — that | | |

## CHECKLIST 5

*Assessment of degree of visual discrimination*

A thorough diagnostic test can be used at a later stage, but an earlier abbreviated form will give a rough guide.

Ask the student which of the shapes on the right of the line is the same as the one on the left.

| | |
|---|---|
| n | m n u w |
| b | p d b q |
| W | A M V W |
| vmp | vnq wnp vmp wmq |
| hqb | byb hqb dyh hpd |
| lwz | lwz sml zlw lms |
| pear | pare pear part peer |
| mael | male maol mael marl |
| peace | paece peace paeec pceae |
| vmonw | wnvom vwonm vmnow vmonw |

## CHECKLIST 6

*Assessment of word recognition*

Your student may not be a complete beginner, but specific patterns of difficulty may be observed.

1. Visual confusions made by early readers:
   - letters   pq  bd  mn  hy  sz  coea  ji
   - words   diary – dairy      goal – gaol
   from – form      was – saw

2. Confusions made by more able readers
   - Reversals: on – no      nip – pin
     net – ten      tap – pat
   - Errors at the beginnings of words, often due to anxiety over the word endings (confusion between <u>b</u>attle – <u>bo</u>ttle)
   - Errors in the middle of words, often due to anxiety over starting words correctly (confusion between m<u>oo</u>n – m<u>oa</u>n)
   - Errors at the ends of words (confusion between pro<u>fess</u> – pro<u>test</u>)

## CHECKLIST 7

*Assessment of the more able student*

1. Can he use a dictionary, catalogue or index?
2. Is he able to summarize what he has read?
3. Can he use charts, maps, graphs and tables?
4. To what extent can he understand and use a limited technical vocabulary which is related to his work, hobby or interests?
5. Is he able to vary his rate of reading according to the

difficulty of the material and his use of it?

## REMEDIES FOR SPECIFIC FAILURES

Having identified the possible reasons for reading failure it is necessary to select exercises to help correct the problems. Here are some suggestions:

### Guidelines for constructing the contents of a programme

1. Always build up the student's confidence and self image. Avoid frustration.
2. Start at a level well below that which he is able to cope with.
3. Do not attempt to begin to teach reading skills unless he has mastered all of the reading readiness activities (see check list 3 pp. 14-15).

### 4. *Visual skills:*

● If he has difficulty in discriminating between shapes, use games involving matching shapes, and later on letters, such as snap, dominoes and lotto (see pp. 24-25).
In conversation encourage your student to describe objects, using words such as round, square, etc.
Work towards exercises involving matching the shape on the left with one of the four on the right − e.g., T/L T H E. Do similar exercises involving the use of numbers.
Construct these and other exercises, based on the tests given on pp. 14-16. Remember that the student is not yet *reading*, and it is not necessary to identify shapes by letter name.
● Make a sorting tray, initially of single letters, then letter pairs and then three letters. Repeat these activities together with snap, dominoes and lotto using common word-beginnings, endings, plural forms and very short words. Always write clearly, using lower case letters.
● Write the letter t on a card and ask for all the letters which are the same in a short passage to be underlined.
Repeat the exercise by underling all the words which begin with b, etc., and extend to finding words ending in e, ing, ed, ll, etc.
● Left to right orientation. Construct mazes similar to the Moyle examples (see p. 15). Remember to use only left to right and up and down movements. *Never* use right to left movements. Write words, phrases, etc., which your student is able to recognize, on a roll of paper one inch wide. Then allow the

writing to unroll, emphasizing the movement of the eye to the right.

● Practise putting a sentence of about five words into correct sequence.

● Practise putting a series of pictures into their correct order.

● Help difficulties of recall by asking the student to repeat phrases and very short sentences and stories. Ask for simple instructions to be carried out.

● Develop language by talking with and reading short passages to your student. Discuss what you have read. Show an object and ask him to select the correct description from four possibles. Allow him to play with a tape recorder and get to know the sound of his voice and language.

## 5. *Auditory skills:*

● Practise repeating clapped rhythms and identifying recorded sounds.

● Exaggerate differences in sounds. Read out word pairs.
Slowly involve finer discrimination between the words used.

Question 1. Are both words the same or are they different?

| | |
|---|---|
| cat — dog | patch — patch |
| bite — bite | port — sport |
| many — few | pan — tan |

Question 2. Is the first sound you hear in each word the same or is it different?

| | |
|---|---|
| man — man | bat — pat |
| gun — fire | ferry — very |
| boy — sail | pen — pen |

● Base discrimination exercises on rhyming words:

| | | | |
|---|---|---|---|
| fun | gun | fine | sun |
| sin | shin | skin | slim |

● Extend the period of memory required by increasing selection lists to five and later six words.

● Give a word and ask your student to tell you words which are similar in different ways — similar beginning, middle sound, etc.

## 6. *Correction of some reading difficulties:*

*a* Transpositions

Some adults change letter positions in words as a result of too much emphasis being placed on the word ending, e.g. nest — nets. Use exercises in which your student is asked to select one of a pair of words to complete a sentence:

The baby is in its $\begin{matrix} \text{pram} \\ \text{parm} \end{matrix}$.

I $\begin{matrix} \text{drive} \\ \text{dirve} \end{matrix}$ my car to work.

b Starting difficulties

Errors may be made between words whose endings are the same but which begin differently. Make two identical lists of about six to eight words, all of which should have the same ending but with different beginnings. Number the words. Read out the words from your list, and ask your student to say the number of the word, from his list, as each word is read. Later read a number and ask your student to say the word.

| | | | |
|---|---|---|---|
| 1. | common | 4. | summon |
| 2. | poison | 5. | stilton |
| 3. | crampon | 6. | reason |

c Word ending difficulties

Use the same system as in b above, using words where the first few letters are the same but which have different endings:

| | | | |
|---|---|---|---|
| 1. | profess | 4. | protrude |
| 2. | provide | 5. | promote |
| 3. | protest | 6. | prohibit |

d Difficulties with the middles of words:

Use the words-in-sentences method as in a above:

Please $\begin{matrix} \text{lack} \\ \text{lock} \end{matrix}$ the front door.

There was a bright $\begin{matrix} \text{moon} \\ \text{moan} \end{matrix}$ last night.

e Word reversals

Again use the words-in-sentences method:

The cloth is $\begin{matrix} \text{on} \\ \text{no} \end{matrix}$ the table.

He caught the rabbit in a $\begin{matrix} \text{part} \\ \text{trap} \end{matrix}$.

It is important to emphasize left to right patterns when working with this difficulty.

7. Examples of aids which you can make to help with early reading difficulties are given on pages 24-25.

# THE LANGUAGE EXPERIENCE METHOD

When starting to teach a student to read, this has been found to be one of the best methods (see linguistic method p. 8).

## Equipment required

Two cards, each measuring about 30cm x 24cm and ruled with pencil lines about 3cm apart
A pencil
Two black fibre-tipped pens
A pair of scissors
A scribbling pad
Two foolscap envelopes
Some paste or glue

## Method

1. Talk with your student about anything which interests him. Jot down on your pad about ten of his phrases.
2. Read back the phrases, and agree with him that they are what he has said.
3. Copy the phrases, in pencil, one below the other down one of the cards, using all lower case letters. As you write each word, and complete each phrase, say it aloud and ask him to repeat the word or phrase after you. Help him where he has difficulty.
4. Give him a fibre-tipped pen and ask him to write over your pencilled writing, again repeating the words and phrases as he proceeds. Read, and ask him to repeat the completed card.
5. Quickly make a copy of the card, with a fibre-tipped pen, on the second card.
6. Cut the second card into phrase strips. Shuffle them and ask him to match each strip with his own card. When he has found a phrase which matches ask him to read the strip.
7. When this has been done for all the phrases cover the master card and shuffle the strips. Place them face down between you and your student. Give him one of the envelopes and keep one yourself.
8. Turn over the strips one at a time and ask your student to read the phrase. If he reads it correctly place the strip in his envelope, but if he has difficulty place it in your own.
9. Repeat the matching and reading exercise 6 using the strips in your envelope. Then repeat the envelope exercise 8 until all the strips are in your student's envelope.

10. Let your student paste his card into his book.

11. Cut the strips into separate words and repeat the complete process (steps 6 to 9 above).

12. Repeat this procedure a number of times using different sets of phrases.

## Guidelines for using the language experience method

1. Do not hurry to get the student on to reading books.

2. Take care not to over-emphasize this use of his own interests as a source of material. Your student may become bored and lose interest entirely unless you use a variety of subjects. News items, shared experiences, even the weather, can form the bases of sets of phrases.

3. Extend the phrases into sentences quite quickly.

4. When moving on to phonic work (see next section) use your student's own vocabulary of known words. Introduce new words slowly.

# 3

## PREPHONIC SKILLS

There are a number of ways of teaching phonics. The worst of
these give much attention to drills and rules, ignoring meaning,
interest and involvement in reading. The English language is
irregular, so that it is necessary to be aware that many 'rules'
have exceptions. The tutor should avoid over-emphasizing letter
or word recognition at the expense of reading for meaning.

Printed words are composed of symbols which represent
sounds. These symbols can be letters or groups of letters. Phonic
work involves the identification, sounding and blending of groups
of symbols to form words. The ability to recognize the parts of
an unfamiliar word, sound them individually, and then blend
them to say the word is the basic aim of phonic work. The development of the ability to rhyme is an important part of this work
(see p. 42).

If students are to be able to read independently and have the
ability to unlock new words they must have a grounding in phonic
work. Having said that you must be sure that your student has all
the skills which are necessary for him to gain the maximum value
and understanding from this section of the work. Before starting
phonic work ensure that he has *all* the skills in checklist 8.

## CHECKLIST 8

1. Discrimination between sounds:

    p, t, f, v, n, s

2. The ability to rhyme:

    boy — toy, wall — fall, clear — sneer, due — few

3. To recognize similarities in the sounds and endings of words:

    top — pot, true — blew, man — hand, fry — try

4. The ability to identify and imitate sounds, then to blend the
individual sounds together to form words.

Your student should be able to say distinctly words which contain some of the basic phonic groupings, such as:

| | | | | |
|---|---|---|---|---|
| plan | best | moth | strike | leave |
| screen | black | throne | desk | misty |
| gang | watch | breeze | queen | flow |
| box | they | blot | dawn | pain |

5. The recognition of words out of place in a series:

| | | | | | |
|---|---|---|---|---|---|
| ● | man | cat | *milk* | tap | |
| ● | cat | sit | mat | *fire* | foot |
| ● | kite | fire | *mat* | mike | |
| ● | soon | sun | *fun* | sand | sauce |
| ● | box | *look* | hot | pop | |

6. The ability to see differences and similarities in visual symbols:

b–d, p–q, m–n, w–v, boy–toy, every–very, no–on, may–map

7. Has the student developed a wide speaking vocabulary?
8. Has he developed a fairly good sight vocabulary?(Between 50 and 70 sight words)

## Guidelines for teaching of phonic work

1. Teach with words that are already known.
2. Work with words in relation to the context.
3. Introduce new learning slowly.
4. Supplement phonic work with general reading and comprehension.

## SUGGESTED ORDER FOR TEACHING PHONICS

In the teaching of the phonic approach to word recognition it is important to remember to allow time for silent and/or oral reading from material suitable to the stage you have reached with your student. It is essential to follow up exercises immediately with words in context.

### Guidelines for the planning of the phonic programme

1. Remember to encourage growth of spoken vocabulary.
2. Give practice in the discrimination of different sounds (see checklist 8 p. 22).
3. Teach the names of the letters followed by their sounds:
   *a* Short vowel sounds – a, e, i, o, u (c<u>a</u>t).
   *b* Introduce single consonants. It is possible to sound some consonants on their own, as a pure sound – e.g., m when humming a tune. Other consonants cannot be sounded alone in this way. Most of these are sometimes called plosives, examples are b, d, g, k, p, t. When sounding the consonant b the sound which is usually made is the phoneme or *b* PLUS a

# Pre Reading Activities for Adults

## Dominoes

### SHAPE TO SHAPE

| ○ | △ |

| △ | □ |

| □ | ○ |

### PICTURE TO PICTURE

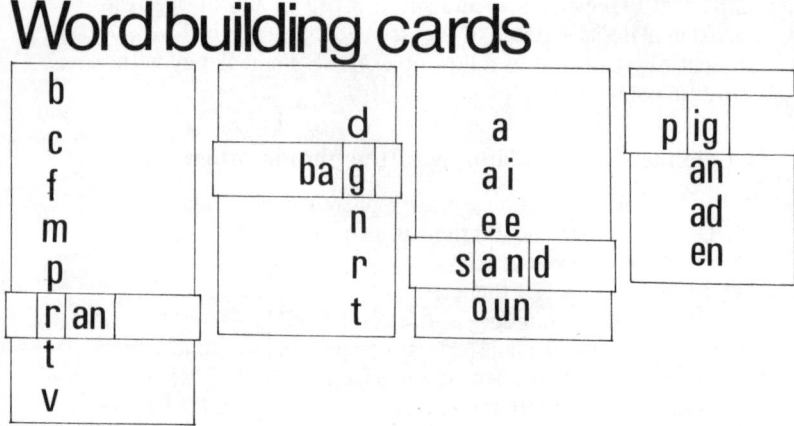

### LETTER TO LETTER

| b | q |

| q | d |

| d | b |

### WORD TO WORD

| cat | tree |

| tree | dog |

| dog | cat |

## Word building cards

b
c
f
m
p
r an
t
v

d
ba g
n
r
t

a
a i
e e
s a n d
o u n

p ig
an
ad
en

# Spinning Words

# Word Wheel

# Anagrams

shif
rete
letket
kclco

# Rotating letter cubes

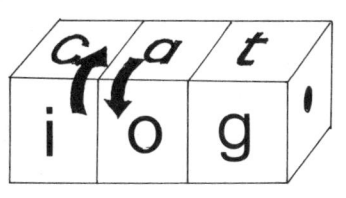

# Clock face game

1 bad
2 din
3 rang
4 thing
5 that
6 apple
7 field
8 fried

9 ever
10 every

11 weight
12 wait

*-uh* sound. It is very difficult to sound the phoneme alone. The consonants are listed, therefore, as those which can, or cannot, be sounded in isolation:

  (i) Those which can be sounded in isolation – f, l, m, n, r, s, v, z

  (ii) Those which cannot be sounded in isolation – b, c, d, g, h, j, k, p, q, t, w, x, y

4.   Start blending consonants with beginnings and endings – ca-t and c-at

5.   Practise listening for, and repeating, beginnings and endings of words.

6.   Provide opportunities to listen for, and repeat, the sound units of words which are known. Make up simple if stilted sentences – e.g., The man travelled through Canada to Alaska (see p. 38).

7.   Teach the double vowels (f-ee-t and s-oo-n)

8.   Teach beginning, middle and ending combinations:

*a*  Beginnings

| br | bl | sh | ch |
|----|----|----|----|
| cr | cl | st | th |
| dr | fl | sp |    |
| fr | gl | sw |    |
| gr | pl |    |    |
| pr | sl |    |    |
| tr |    |    |    |

*b*  Middles

| ai | er | ir | oi | ur |
|----|----|----|----|----|
| ar | ey |    | oy |    |
| ay |    |    | or |    |
|    |    |    | ou |    |

*c*  Endings

| ing | ck | all | sh | ight |
|-----|----|-----|----|----|
| ang | ch | ell | st | ought |
| ong |    | oll |    |    |
| ung |    | ull |    |    |

This takes time and must not be hurried.

9.   Teach the three-letter combinations:

| Beginnings | Endings |
|------------|---------|
| scr | ail |
| spr | oil |
| sch | eat |
| thr | ear |
|     | ink |

10. Teach the 'silent e'.
   Explain that the 'silent e' has effect on vowels only, as in mat − mate, bath − bathe.
11. Silent letters:
   *a* 'Silent b', always at the end of words, as in bomb, limb.
   *b* 'Silent k', 'w' and 'g' are found at the beginning of words, as in knot, write, gnat.
12. Phonic additives:
   *a* Teach 'y' making two different sounds as in happy and cry.
   *b* 'q' is always followed by 'u'.
   *c* 'ough' as in though, bough, through, ought, cough, rough.
   *d* Teach 'ph' as in photograph.
13. Exceptional words which have to be learnt. There are many of these and some examples are:
   *a* 'ch' as in chemist and stomach
   *b* 'mn' as in autumn
   *c* 'some', 'come', etc.
14. Break down and rebuild words into familiar units − e.g., hand-bag, fan-tas-tic.
15. Look at new words, say sound units and blend into the word − e.g., re-hab-il-it-ate.
16. Use context clues in recognizing unphonetic words − e.g., he hit the ball —— the window
17. Teach the relationships between:
   *a* Root words − basic words from which others are built −
   e.g., habit, in-habit, habit-able, un-in-habit-able
   *b* Prefixes: in-, pro-, co-, un-
   *c* Suffixes: -ing, -able, -ious, -itis
Relate this type of analysis to meaning − e.g., in + an adjective negates the adjective: in + accurate, in + capable.
18. Practise writing words, which have a number of phonetic syllables, from dictation − e.g., rep-re-sent.
19. Encourage reading and the use of a dictionary to help with pronunciation and meanings of new words.

## Some useful exercises

Many games and activities can be used to help with all stages in the teaching of phonics. Some examples are:
1. A 'Programmed Reading Kit' developed by D.H. Stott (see p. 38)
2. Variations on 'bingo' using words instead of numbers
3. 'Snap' using words

4. Exercises constructed on the principle being taught:
   *blending* – find the odd man out
       b<u>r</u>ead, b<u>r</u>ing, b<u>r</u>own, down, b<u>r</u>ake
   *double vowel* – put in the missing word
       sh<u>ee</u>p, m<u>ee</u>t, f<u>ee</u>t, k - - p
   *matching* – put these words into families

| cat  | book  | sheet |
|------|-------|-------|
| soot | sheep | mat   |
| meet | look  | rat   |

5. Encourage your student to keep his own 'word families book'. This should take the form of a dictionary based on *sounds* rather than alphabetical letters.

## PHONIC CHECKLIST

A checklist of symbols which are used to represent sounds must be generalized in nature. It is important to remember that the same sound can be written in different ways. Consider the following series:

| t<u>ai</u>l | m<u>ai</u>n | f<u>ay</u> |
|------|------|------|
|      | m<u>oa</u>n |      |
| t<u>i</u>le | m<u>i</u>ne | f<u>ie</u> |
| t<u>ow</u>el |      |      |
| t<u>oi</u>l |      |      |
|      |      | f<u>ea</u>r |
|      |      | f<u>ai</u>r |
|      | m<u>oo</u>r |      |
| t<u>ea</u>l | m<u>ea</u>n | f<u>ee</u> |
| t<u>i</u>ll | m<u>i</u>ni |      |
| t<u>e</u>ll | m<u>e</u>n |      |
|      | m<u>a</u>n |      |
|      |      | f<u>ar</u> |
| t<u>o</u>ll |      |      |
| t<u>a</u>ll | m<u>au</u>l |      |
|      | m<u>u</u>ll |      |
| t<u>oo</u>l | m<u>oo</u>n |      |
|      |      | f<u>ur</u> |

Therefore where a vowel is listed it is essential that all of the variety of sounds which are linked with the vowel be taught.

The following list can be used to check that the main phonic rules have been covered.

# CHECKLIST 9

1. Vowels: a, e, i, o, u
2. Consonants:
   *a* which can be sounded in isolation (see p. 26)
   　f, l, m, n, r, s, v, z
   *b* which cannot be sounded in isolation (see p. 26)
   　b, c, d, g, h, j, k, p, q, t, w, x, y
3. Double consonants: bb, dd, ff, gg, ll, ss, tt, ck
4. Consonant digraphs* ch, gh, kn (k silent), ng, ph, sh, th, tch,
   　　　　　　　　　　　wh, wr, qu
5. Consonant blends:

   | | | | |
   |---|---|---|---|
   | bl | br | cl | cr |
   | dr | dw | fl | fr |
   | gl | gr | pl | pr |
   | sc | scr | sh | shr |
   | sk | sl | sm | sn |
   | sp | spl | spr | squ |
   | st | str | sw | thr |
   | tr | tw | | |

6. Vowel diphthongs*: ai, au, ea, ee, ei, eu, ie,
   　　　　　　　　　　oa, oe, oi, oo, ou, ue
7. Murmur diphthongs* or vowels modified by r: ar, er, ir, or, ur
8. Vowel digraphs:

   | | |
   |---|---|
   | ah – ah | ey – they |
   | aw – paw | oh – oh |
   | ay – say | ow – flow, now |
   | eh – eh | oy – boy |
   | ew – few, sew | |

9. c followed by e, i, or y makes a soft s sound
   g followed by e, i, or y makes a soft j sound
   s makes a z sound in has

10. The final 'silent e':
   *a* Functionless – as in jungle, kettle, noise
   *b* Modifies – makes preceding vowel longer as in can cane,
   pan pane
   *c* Special pronunciation – are in f-are
   　　　　　　　　　　　　　ire in f-ire
   　　　　　　　　　　　　　ure in p-ure

# PHONIC ASSESSMENT TEST

It is important to assess carefully and regularly the phonic structures which the student has learnt, and those which need further practice. The 207 words are arranged in 3 sections. Section 1 contains most of the sounds represented by vowels and their combinations (see p. 29) in the beginning and middle positions. Section 2 contains most of the sounds represented by consonants, and their combinations, (see p. 29) in the beginning, middle, and ending positions. Section 3 contains the most common endings. The structure representing the sound being tested is underlined in each word. Only this part of the word need be sounded correctly for the word to be marked correct. In each section the letter arrangements within the words become progressively more difficult. Sounds which are made incorrectly, or not at all, should be noted. Further exercises which include these words should be done with your student before retesting. It is important not to omit structures which have been correctly sounded from exercises if all of the common letter patterns are to be learnt thoroughly by the student.

## *Method*

The student is asked to read the words at his own speed. Errors in pronunciation are noted and listed for work in the future. Words are identified by the line number and column letter. Thus in the first list ace is referred to as 2B and book as 4D. The tutor should not say anything whilst the student is doing the test, but merely note mistakes or difficulties.

## Sounds represented by vowels

|     | A     | B    | C       | D     |
|-----|-------|------|---------|-------|
| 1.  | task  | cat  | do      | hide  |
| 2.  | bed   | ace  | machine | be    |
| 3.  | rare  | bid  | old     | watch |
| 4.  | done  | rope | food    | book  |
|     |       |      |         |       |
| 5.  | fort  | boil | moor    | blood |
| 6.  | tune  | few  | toy     | clout |
| 7.  | bird  | sun  | now     | soup  |
| 8.  | clerk | war  | purr    | mar   |

| 9. | fair | her | calm | saw |
| 10. | fur | great | cheese | height |
| 11. | pay | taught | dead | laugh |
| 12. | bear | tail | each | nought |
| 13. | sew | seize | country | pure |
| 14. | field | boat | feud | eight |
| 15. | they | cough | shoe | due |
| 16. | low | does | fall | doe |
| 17. | end | tour | tie | cause |
| 18. | iris | use | unfold | income |
| 19. | open | active | eel | |

## Sounds represented by consonants

| | A | B | C | D | E |
|---|---|---|---|---|---|
| 1. | let | rat | sang | not | fun |
| 2. | zip | vase | met | bed | cut |
| 3. | get | jar | hall | dole | keg |
| 4. | past | told | yawn | win | queen |
| 5. | wreck | enough | sight | lurch | naughty |
| 6. | knife | roughen | ring | chair | |
| 7. | lack | worship | path | where | shop |
| 8. | phone | notch | wash | watcher | that |
| 9. | bubble | clown | crow | drop | flop |
| 10. | adrift | blot | dwell | brim | include |
| 11. | comprise | implied | frame | glare | afflict |
| 12. | ingrown | haggle | plot | grey | confront |
| 13. | price | slap | escape | shred | scram |
| 14. | mask | scan | enshrine | describe | skate |
| 15. | dislodge | spray | aspic | spot | parsnip |
| 16. | small | splash | rasp | spasm | snake |
| 17. | steam | sweet | restring | square | fast |
| 18. | esplanade | enthral | straw | esquire | throw |
| 19. | twist | entrance | entwine | tripe | castle |
| 20. | gnome | haunt | action | | |
| 21. | fern | bomb | orphan | held | |
| 22. | rink | ghost | write | choir | |

31

## Sounds represented by endings

|    | A        | B        | C        | D    | E    |
|----|----------|----------|----------|------|------|
| 1. | patting  | rider    | fated    |      |      |
| 2. | walls    | miles    | worries  |      |      |
| 3. | baby     | fly      | wedge    |      |      |
| 4. | marked   | carried  | smallest | able |      |
| 5. | manly    | awful    | plough   | sink |      |
| 6. | sail     | soil     | seat     | near | seer |
| 7. | election | relation | tension  |      |      |
| 8. | final    | finality |          |      |      |

## SPELLING RULES

Among students with reading problems difficulties with vocabulary, speech and spelling occur more often than any others. Literacy students will probably make more than five times as many spelling errors as others of similar age. The largest proportion of these errors tend to be reversals.

In dealing with spelling difficulties it is essential that the tutor avoids over-criticizing. It is not necessary to correct *every* spelling error in written work. I find that more sucessful teaching can come from never writing anything on a student's work. I make a carbon copy of my comments so that both my student and I have a copy.

When a student who has real spelling difficulties is reading or writing, he may need to make frequent stops to puzzle out individual words. This can break the flow of his thoughts and destroy any clues which the context may give.

Accurate spelling is therefore essential if the student is to read and write freely and without hesitation. The rules, like phonic work, must be taught carefully, thoroughly and systematically. However, the same care must be taken to avoid total concentration on this one element of the work to the exclusion of general reading and comprehension, as was emphasized with phonic work.

### Some reasons for spelling problems:

1.  Visual — ● Perception of words(see pp. 11, 16)
    ● Discrimination of symbols (see checklist 8 (6) p. 23)
    ● Span of perception (eye movements as described on pp. 11-12)
2.  Auditory — difficulty in the analysis of word sounds

3. Pronunciation difficulties and differences in dialect
4. Inattention to detail
5. Poor memory and difficulties with recall (see checklist 3 (3) and (7) pp. 14-15)


## CHECKLIST 10

1.  q is always written as qu. It never stands by itself: quick, queen, quarrel.
2.  No English words end in the letters v or j.

    v —    always add 'silent e'
            drive, have, give

    j —    the following combinations are used for this sound:
            ge as in rage
            dge as in badge

3.  Double l, f and s after a single short vowel at the end of a word: sell, fill, stiff, duff, mass, loss.

    Exceptions are well-known sight words: pal, if, bus, nil, of, gas, this, yes.

4.  Regular plurals are made by adding s: animals, horses, cliffs.
5.*a* the sound ee at the end of a word is spelled y, as in baby, happy.

    Exceptions — committee, coffee, see, spaghetti, taxi, (short for taxicab).

  *b* The sound i at the end of a word is made by the letter y as in cry, fly.

    Exceptions — pie, tie, sigh

6.*a* A 'silent e' on the end of a word makes the vowel in front say it's own alphabetical name, as in hate, ride, cube, bake, shire, mere, lobe.

    Exceptions — done, come, give, have

  *b* Drop the 'silent e' when adding an ending which begins with a vowel: make + ing = making
            write + ing = writing
            fate + ed = fated

  *c* If a word ends with a consonant its spelling is usually unchanged when adding an ending which begins with a vowel.
            think + ing = thinking
            feel + ing = feeling

7.  If a one-syllable word ends with ONE vowel and ONE consonant double the final consonant before adding an ending.
        stop stopped stopping
        flat flatter flattest

Exceptions — fix, box, where the x is counted as a double consonant.

8.   The endings ck, dge, tch follow a short vowel that does not say its name: pick, track, dodge, badge, latch, patch.

9.   i before e except after c or in words sounding a long a as in weigh, eight.

   Exceptions — either, neither, weird, height, seize.

10.  Words ending with a consonant + y
     Change the y to i before adding any ending *except* ing.
          party — parties, marry — married
     BUT cry — crying

11.  When w comes before or it says wer as in worship, work.
     Exceptions — worry, worried, worn

12.  When c is followed by e, i or y it says s as in centre, circles.
     Otherwise it says k as in cottage, cream.

13.  When g is followed by e, i or y it says j as in gentle, giant, gypsum.
     Otherwise it is hard as in gold, gallon, guide
     Exceptions — get, girl, give, gear, giddy

14.  ti, ci and si all say sh at the beginning of all syllables except the first, as in nation, gracious, mansion.

15.  all and well followed by another syllable only have one l as in already, welcome.

16.  full and till joined to a root word drop one l as in useful, until.

17.  Words ending in l after a single vowel double the l before adding an ending.
          cancel — cancelling
          metal — metallic

18.  -ceed -sede -cede
     There are 3 words ending in -ceed — succeed exceed proceed
          1 word ending in -sede — supersede
     All others are -cede — intercede precede

19.  *Plurals*

●   If a word ends in one of the following sounds:— s, x, z, sh, ch, add es to form plurals —
          buses, foxes, buzzes, dishes, churches

●   Some words are alike in singular and plural —
          deer, sheep

●   If a word ends in o preceded by a consonant add es —
          potato, potatoes
     If ending in o preceded by a vowel usually add s —
          radio, radios

●     Words ending in ey add s but words ending in a consonant
followed by y drop the y and add ies —
>    monkey — monkeys
>    cherry — cherries

●     Nouns ending in f change the f to v before adding es —
>    leaf — leaves

Exceptions — dwarfs, roofs, chiefs

●     Some plurals just have to be learnt —
>    child — children, foot — feet, mouse — mice

20.  *Suffix and prefix*

●     When a prefix is added to a word its basic spelling remains
the same —
>    un-clean, dis-obey, mis-take

●     When a suffix is added most root words remain unchanged
except for those ending in y or e —
>    care — caring, hurry — hurried

21.  *Homonyms*

Words which sound alike but have different meanings, and
frequently different spellings, are known as homonyms. These
words are often the cause of great difficulty and embarrassment
to adults.
>    week — weak, heal — heel, pair — pear

# 4

## BOOKS FOR USE WITH STUDENTS

For an explanation of the Scale numbers see page 9

*Scale 1 to 7*

| | | |
|---|---|---|
| Trend | The Dark House | Ginn |
| | Wild Dog | |
| Ladybird | Keyword Easy Readers – Series 643 (6 titles) | Wills & Hepworth |
| | Keyword Reading Scheme – Books 1 to 4 | |

*Scale 7 to 8·5*

| | | |
|---|---|---|
| Teenage Twelve | Books 3 to 8 | Gibson |
| Inner Ring Books | 1st series (12 titles) | Benn |
| Trend | Sudden Death | Ginn |
| | Watcher on the Wharf | |
| | Old Bootleg | |
| | A Real Hero | |
| | Robbie | |
| Ladybird | Keyword Reading Scheme – Books 5 to 7 | Wills & Hepworth |
| | Leaders – Series 737 (6 titles) | |
| ――――― | Ants | Angus & Robertson |
| | The Bee | |
| | Cooking is Fun | |
| Tempo Books | The Swinging Kings | Longman |
| | The Big Drop | |
| | Lost in the Fog | |
| Sound Sense Readers | Books 1 to 3 | E.J. Arnold |

*Scale 8·5 to 9·5*

| | | |
|---|---|---|
| Teenage Twelve | Books 9 to 12 | Gibson |
| Inner Ring Books | Second series (12 books) | Benn |
| Trend | Coffee at Charlie's | Ginn |
| | Bindi Eye | |
| | Crash Landing | |
| | Gaye Lizzie | |

| | | |
|---|---|---|
| Ladybird | Keyword Reading Scheme — Books 8 to 10 | Wills & Hepworth |
| | People at Work (20 titles) | |
| | Games (2 titles) | |
| | Through the Ages (2 titles) | |
| | Easy Geography (3 titles) | |
| | Nature — Pets, Wild Animals (19 titles) | |
| They Were First | 12 titles | Oliver & Boyd |
| Famous Ships | 4 titles | Oliver & Boyd |
| Discovery Readers | Books 4 to 11 | Harrap |
| Tempo Books | Books 5 to 10 | Longman |
| Fun and Adventure | 2 books | Macmillan |
| True Adventure Series | 33 books | Blackie |
| Sound Sense | Books 4 to 6 | E.J. Arnold |

*Scale 9·5 to 14*

| | | |
|---|---|---|
| Topliner Series | 15 titles | Macmillan |
| Ann and Jenny Books | 6 books (suitable for women up to about 23 yrs of age) | Ginn |
| Jet Books | Books 1 to 12 | Cape |
| Booster Books | The Man from Mars | Heinemann |
| | The Gomez Story | |
| | H.M.S. Thing | |
| | The Spider Bomb | |
| New Worlds to Conquer | 5 books | Chambers |
| Trend Books | Cry on a Foggy Night | Ginn |
| | Snow at Tataru | |
| Sound Sense | Books 7 and 8 | E.J. Arnold |

## Reading Schemes

Whilst it has been said that it is not advisable to work through a single scheme, it is important that some *complete* schemes are available and that a programme is constructed using parts of a number of different ones.

Schemes which have sections which are especially helpful in working with adults are:

*Breakthrough to Literacy,* Longman.
Wordmaker and Sentence Maker material.
*Lively Reading*, Nelson.
4 kits consisting in each case of a workbook and 4 readers
*New Stott Learning Kit,* Holmes McDougall.
The Pattern of English Kit and the sections dealing with handwriting, spelling and sentence building

## Phonically structured schemes

*Royal Road Readers*, Chatto and Windus
A series of 9 books, with companion books, 5 question books and a teacher's book
*Sound Sense Readers*, E.J. Arnold
Books 1 to 8 (see scales above)

## The Ladybird Scheme

*Keyword Reading Scheme* (Books 1 to 12) with a projected Reading Scale progression from 5·0 to 10·4.
The structure of the scheme is as follows:

300 KEYWORDS

| 250 WORD BASIC LIST | 50 RESERVE WORDS |
|---|---|
| 1934 WORD VOCABULARY | |
| INTRODUCTION OF NEW WORDS AT A LOW RATE | HIGH REPETITION |

NEW WORDS CARRY OVER FROM STAGE TO STAGE UNTIL STAGE 8

3 books in each stage with a similar structure in each case:
  1a  16 words repeated 10 times per word
  1b  the same 16 words with different context and pictures
  1c  the same 16 words with different context and pictures plus 4 instructional words

The Ladybird Scheme can be used as the basis of a programme for an adult student. Tutors generally find that it is useful to introduce more formal phonic work at about book 5.

## General

*Learning to Spell* by Martyn and Brook, Harper
    A useful book, although care must be taken to select the
    sections which are most appropriate for the adult student's use.
*The Harrap Spelling Books* by K. Anderson, Harrap
    Again, care must be taken in the books 1 and 2. Most of the
    material in books 3 and 4 is very suitable for use with adults.

## SOME SOURCES OF INTEREST MATERIAL

A number of large companies and national industries have educational departments. These can be contacted, and requests made for copies of their publications for schools. It is important to mention that one is teaching a student who is interested in the products of the company. Examples of this type of material are:

| | |
|---|---|
| *The Story of Rubber* | Dunlop |
| *The Story of the Wheel* | |
| *Radio and the Post Office* | The Post Office |
| *Ring Around the World* | |
| *How Matches are Made* | Bryant and May |
| *How a Chequebook Works* | Midland Bank |

It can also be useful to ask for recruiting material for posts at all levels in the company or industry. Any large company can be approached. Some suggestions are given below:

British Airways, Speedbird House, London Airport, Heathrow
Avon Rubber Co. Ltd, Melksham, Wiltshire FN12 8AA
Barclays Bank Ltd, 54 Lombard St, London EC3P 3AH
British Aircraft Corporation, 100 Pall Mall, London SW1 5HR
British Leyland Ltd, Leyland House, Marylebone Rd, London NW1 5AA
British Petroleum Co. Ltd, Brittannic House, Moor Lane, London EC2Y 9BU
British Railways Board, 222 Marylebone Rd, London NW1 6JJ

British Sugar Bureau, 140 Park Lane, London W1Y 3AA
Burmah Castrol Co. Ltd, Pipers Way, Swindon, Wilts, SN3 1RE
Cadbury Schweppes Ltd, 2-10 Connaught Place, Marble Arch, London W2 2EX
The Dunlop Co. Ltd, 10-12 King St, London SW1 Y6RA
Ford Motor Co. Ltd, Eagle Way, Warley, Nr Brentwood, Essex CM13 3BW
Fisons Ltd, Agro-Chemical Division, Harston, Cambridge
I.C.I., Imperial Chemicals House, Millbank, London SW1 P3JF
Michelin Tyre Co. Ltd, Campbell Rd, Stoke on Trent, Staffs ST4 4EY
Lloyds Bank Ltd, 10 Lombard St, London EC3V 9EE
Midland Bank Ltd, P.O. Box 125, Poultry, London EC2 2BX
National Coal Board, Hobart House, Grosvenor Place, London SW1X 7AE
National Westminster Bank Ltd, National Westminster House, 326-333 High Holborn, London WC1V 7QA
Pilkington Bros Ltd, St Helens, Lancs
The Post Office, Central Headquarters, 23 Howland St, London W1P 6HQ
Rank's, Hovis, McDougall Ltd, RHM Centre, 152 Grosvenor Rd, London SW1V 3JL
Rolls-Royce Ltd, P.O. Box 31, Derby DE2 8BJ
Rowntree Mackintosh Ltd, Wigginton Rd, York YO1 1XY
Shell Group, Shell Centre, London SE1 7NA
Tate & Lyle Ltd, 21 Mincing Lane, London EC3R 7QY
Vauxhall Motors Ltd, Kimpton Rd, Luton, Beds LU2 0SY
Watney Mann Ltd, Palace St, London SW1
Woodall-Duckham Ltd, Woodall-Duckham House, The Boulevard, Crawley, Sussex

## SPECIFIC INTEREST BOOKS

Assess the readability (see p. 9) of the section which you are planning to use, to ensure that it is suitable for your student.

### Cars

*The AA Book of the Car*, Drive Publications
Large clear drawings, diagrams and photographs; writing split into short sections; generally informative.
*The Shell book of How Cars Work*, Shellmex and B.P.
Well illustrated; longer written passages; uses more technical

language which it assumes the reader will understand.
*The Highway Code*, H.M.S.O.
Essential for new drivers; very often the 'first book' actually read.
*Workshop Manuals*
Those by J.H. Haynes, Odcombe Press, Yeovil are recommended.
For the real expert or enthusiast; published for specific car
models; step by step instructions and likely problems mentioned;
photographs and large 'exploded' diagrams.

## Football

*Inswingers* by Gregory and Ward, Hulton Books
A series of 6 books about a young man who leaves school early
to join a football club.

## Gardening

*Be Your Own Expert series* Pan Britannica Industries Ltd
4 books on Gardening, Lawns, Roses, Houseplants; many useful
colour illustrations.
*The Gardening Year* Readers Digest Association
For the student who is really interested in gardening; well
written and illustrated; short passages; step by step instructions
throughout the year: an excellent book.
*Simple Greenhouse Gardening* Ward Locke
For the slightly more knowledgeable student. Diagrams and
photographs; longish sections of writing.

## Children

It is difficult to find a 'Baby Book' which uses a restricted
vocabulary without talking down to the reader.
*Young Student's Book of Child Care* by L. Pitcairn, C.U.P.
The language level is reasonable for an early reader but care must
be taken in using this book as the values which it assumes may
not be the same as those of your students. Some photographs.
*This is Your Body* by M.R. Delaney, Macmillan
A reasonable book with some 'word missing' exercises. It covers
all aspects of Human Biology, with illustrations, and has short
passages which can be used with a very early reader.
*Good Housekeeping Baby Book* by Dr. J. Voster, Ebury Press.
The language used would indicate use with the more able reader,
but the clearly numbered, short paragraphs make it possible for it

to be used quite early on. A 'dip into' book rather than for straight reading.

## Do-it-Yourself

*Better Homes, Handyman's Book*, Book Club Associates
Very well illustrated with numerous photographs. Short written sections make this book suitable for the very early reader, *but* some basic practical knowledge is required.

## Cookery

There are numerous cookery books available and every housewife will have her favourite. I have found the following useful with students who have reading problems:
*Easy Cooking for One or Two* Penguin
This book is based on the work at the Geriatric Research Unit and is very suitable for many of our students. The meals are relatively cheap to produce and a section for non-cooks is included. This book is set in a large, clear type, and stage-by-stage instructions are given.
*Hamlyn All Colour Cookbook* Hamlyn
For the more accomplished cook and the reader of slightly higher ability. Illustrated with colour photographs. Includes 300 quick tips for cooks.

## General

Rhyming work as a preparation for the phonic section of the programme is important (see pp. 22 ff.). But the whole area of poetry as a part of literature in general must not be omitted. I have known a number of students who have had great difficulty in writing prose but who have been able to produce poems of length and variety. These works often showed a degree of insight which was quite remarkable. It would be wrong therefore to assume that all the student wishes to read is prose related to interest. He has probably missed the fun of playing with words and ideas, and the whole rich world of the poet.
*Passport to Poetry series 1 to 4* by E.L. Black & D.S. Davies, Cassell
*A Puffin Book of Verse* edited by Eleanor Graham, Puffin Books
*The Faber Book of Modern Verse* edited by M. Roberts, Faber & Faber (Paperback) — for the more advanced student.

Students who have made a reasonable amount of progress, and have done some phonic work, can use books in the 'Observer's series', published by Warne. The 40 books in this series cover a wide variety of subjects from Birds to Dogs, Aircraft to Music, and Weather to Churches. Books in this series provide a good introduction to work with a dictionary.

Ladybird books are referred to on p. 38. It should be noted that a number of books are produced in this series for a reading level of 9·5+ and over (see p. 9).

| Series | 536 | Nature — Wild Animals |
|---|---|---|
| | 706 | Scouting — 2 titles |
| | 733 | Mythology — 1 title |
| | 691 | Animals of the World — 7 titles |
| | 727 | Conservation — 2 titles |
| | 682 | Animal History — 2 titles |
| | 671 | Understanding Maps |
| | 663 | Our Land in the Making — 2 titles |
| | 651 | Natural History — 6 titles |
| | 654 | How it Works — 14 titles |
| | 601 | Achievements — 24 titles |
| | 662 | Music and Drama — 6 titles |
| | 701 | Art — 3 titles |
| | 584 | Recognition — 5 titles |

The series 684 book on Handwriting is also most useful for both tutor's and student's use.

## General Material

It is useful for the literacy tutor to build up a large collection of written material.

1. Newspaper colour supplements
2. Headlines of different sizes, length and of upper and lower case letters, cut from newspapers
3. Menus
4. Application forms — driving licence renewal; car tax renewal; T.V. and dog licence; social security forms; jobs; hire purchase; holidays and other bookings; insurance proposal forms.
5. Brochures, instruction booklets, guarantees of all kinds
6. Advertisements, under different headings, from newspapers
7. Contracts of employment, and contracts for other services such as house improvements, supply of goods, etc.
8. Income tax forms and guide sheets
9. Telephone directories

10. Radio and TV Times
11. Bank forms: paying-in slips, statements, etc.
12. Bus and train time-tables
13. Car documents — M.O.T. certificates, insurance certificates, etc.

It is a good idea to keep a carrier-bag in the kitchen into which instructions, warnings, contents lists, etc., cut from various packets and labels, can be collected.

These materials are easier to handle if they are either covered with transparent film or a clear plastic folder or bag, or mounted on paper and then covered as appropriate. It is then possible to write on the material and to remove the writing afterwards.

## BOOKS FOR TUTORS

### Progress assessment

A number of tests are available for the assessment of reading. Most use a scale of progress but it is most important to always use the same test when assessing progress and making comparisons.

1. *Neale Analysis of Reading Ability* This test is intended for children with reading levels of 4 to 14·5 (see p. 9) but can be used with adults.

2. *Harrison Stroud Reading Readiness Profiles* An American test in 6 sections, intended primarily for use with children.

    Using symbols
    Making visual discriminations
    Using the context
    Making auditory discriminations
    Using context and auditory clues
    Giving the names of letters

3. *Burt (rearranged) Word Reading Test* This is a basic test of word recognition.

4. *N.F.E.R. Verbal and English Tests*

    Verbal Reasoning series — Tests BC, CD, EF, and GH cover approximately levels 4·5 to 15·0.

    Reading series — Tests BD and EH 1-3 cover approximately levels 7·5 to 16·5.

    English Comprehension — English Progress Tests A2, C2, E2, F2 and G cover levels 4·0 to 17·0.

    These three series of tests are most useful in covering three aspects of reading ability using a wide variety of questioning techniques. The levels given above relate to the assessment of the reading level in adults page 9. The test manuals include norms for all of the tests in terms of childrens' ages.

5. *Daniels and Diack*

The diagnostic tests Nos. 2 to 12 to be found in *The Standard Reading Tests* by J.C. Daniels and Hunter Diack, Chatto and Windus, 1958.

These tests make the testing of a number of pre- and early reading skills possible (see pp. 14-17).

# TUTOR'S BIBLIOGRAPHY

A handbook of this sort can only deal very briefly with the vast, complex subject of adult reading. There may be a number of areas which you will now want to look at in more detail. Some of the following books may be of interest.

| | | |
|---|---|---|
| BALDWIN, G., CARTER, H.L.J. & McGINNIS, D.J. | *Patterns of Sound Diagnosis and Treatment of the Disabled Reader* | Chartwell Press 1969 Collier-Macmillan 1970 |
| DANIELS, J.C., & Hunter DIACK., | *The Royal Road Readers Teacher's Book* | Chatto & Windus 1967 |
| | *The Standard Reading Tests* | Chatto & Windus 1958 |
| DURKIN, Dolores., | *Phonics and The Teaching of Reading* | N.Y. Bureau of Publications, Teachers College, Columbia University 1965 |
| FLESCH, R., | *Why Johnny Can't Read: And What You Can Do About it.* | Harper and Row 1955 |
| GILLILAND, J. & MERRITT, J.E., | *Readability* | U.L.P. 1972 |
| HUGHES, J. | *Phonics and the Teaching of Reading* | Evans Bros. 1972 |
| | *Reading with Phonics* | Evans Bros. 1972 |
| | *Reading and Reading Failures* | Evans Bros. 1972 |
| JONES, W.R. | *Step Up and Read* | U.L.P. 1965 |
| KELLMER-PRINGLE, M.L., | *Deprivation and Education* | Longman 1971 |
| KENNEDY, E.C., | *Methods in Teaching Developmental Reading* | Peacock Publishers, Itasca, Illinois 1974 |
| LEWIS, M.M., | *Language Thought & Personality in Infancy & Childhood* | Harrap 1963 |

| MACKAY & Others, | *Breakthrough to Literacy: Teacher's Manual* | Longman for Schools Council 1970 |
| MONROE, M., | *Children Who Cannot Read* | University of Chicago Press 1932 |
| MORRIS, R., | *Success and Failure in Learning to Read* | Penguin 1973 |
| MOYLE, D., | *The Teaching of Reading* | Ward Locke Educational 1968 |
| MURRAY, W., | *Ladybird Keyword Reading Scheme* | Wills & Hepworth 1971 |
| PETERS, M., | *Spelling: Caught or Taught* | Routledge & Kegan Paul 1967 |
| SCHONELL, F.J., | *The Psychology and Teaching of Reading* | Oliver & Boyd 1961 |
| SOUTHGATE, V. & ROBERTS, G.R., | *Reading, Which Approach?* | U.L.P. 1970 |
| STOTT, D.H., | *Programmed Reading Kit* | Holmes McDougall 1972 |
| STRANG, R. & Others., | *Improvement of Reading* | McGraw-Hill 1967 |
| TANSLEY, A.E., | *Reading and Remedial Reading* | Routledge & Kegan Paul 1967 |
| WILSON, R.M., | *Diagnostic and Remedial Reading for Classroom and Clinic* | I.E.S., C.E. Merrill, Columbus, Ohio 1967 |
| ZINTZ, M.V., | *The Reading Process: The Teacher & the Learner* | Wm. C. Brown Co. U.S.A. 1970 |

# GLOSSARY

**Astigmatism** An uneveness in the surface of the cornea, or clear window at the front of the eye, through which rays of light pass. This can lead to a distorted image being formed.

**Auditory** Relating to sound and hearing.

**Blends** In relation to phonic work (see p. 22) blending is the action of sounding individual letters to form regular groups — e.g., s+t+r and n+g. The regular groups are then blended together using one or more vowels, to form words — e.g., str+i+ng.

**Digraph** Two letters which are grouped together, but making one sound — e.g., th and sh. Vowel digraphs consist of a vowel + a consonant which together make one sound — e.g., ay and ow.

**Diphthong** Two vowels which are grouped together making one sound — e.g., ae, ee, oi. A murmur diphthong is a vowel which is grouped with a letter r. The sound of the r is changed by the vowel — e.g., ar, or, ur.

**Flashing** This is a teaching method which is used in the look-and-say approach. Words are printed in large letters on 'flash cards'. A the card is shown to students, the word is spoken aloud. The student learns to associate the pattern of the word with its sound

**i.t.a.** This represents the initial teaching alphabet. Specially constructed symbols, each indicating a different phonic sound, are used. Many more symbols must be learnt than there are letters in the conventional alphabet. The student learns to sound and decod unfamiliar words quickly and easily, but the change to the conver tional alphabet sometimes causes difficulties.

**Motivation** The force which urges a person to do something. It may be that a student who wants to pass his driving test must als learn to read the Highway Code. So this wish to pass the test could be his motivation for learning to read.

**Phonic Structures** Groups of letters which can be sounded together, and blended to form a word — e.g., ch and ant are phonic structures, xp and jl are not.

**Reading Age** Tests for the assessment of reading ability are usually designed for use with children. Tables supplied with the tests give examples of the marks that children of different ages have scored. The test score can be directly related to the age of the child and referred to as the Reading Age.

**Sight words** These are words which do not represent any real object, and which can only be learnt by seeing the shape of the word and saying its sound. These are sometimes called service words — e.g., and, there, but, for.